How to Draw
Pets

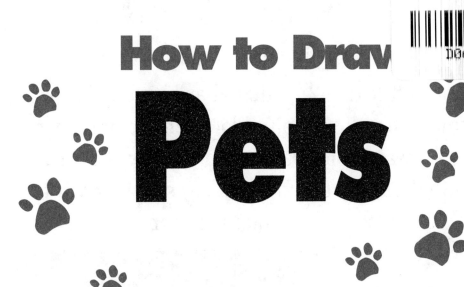

by Linda Murray
illustrated by Janice Kinnealy

Murray, Linda, (date)
    How to draw pets / by Linda Murray; illustrated by Janice Kinnealy.
    p.   cm.
    ISBN 0-8167-2742-2 (lib. bdg.)   ISBN 0-8167-2743-0 (pbk.)
    1. Animals in art—Juvenile literature.   2. Drawing—Technique—
Juvenile literature.   [1. Animals in art.   2. Drawing—Technique.]
I. Kinnealy, Janice, ill.   II. Title.
NC780.M87   1995
743'.6—dc20   94-47279

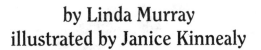

© 1995 by Watermill Press, an imprint of Troll Associates, Inc.

Printed in the United States of America.

10 9 8 7 6 5 4 3 2 1

Watermill Press

Materials

Gather these materials before you begin:

•soft lead (#2) pencil •hard lead (#6H) pencil
•fine- to medium-point black felt-tip marker •crayons
• watercolor paints and paintbrush •eraser
•8$\frac{1}{2}$" x 11" (21.5 cm x 28 cm) sheets of white paper
•tracing paper

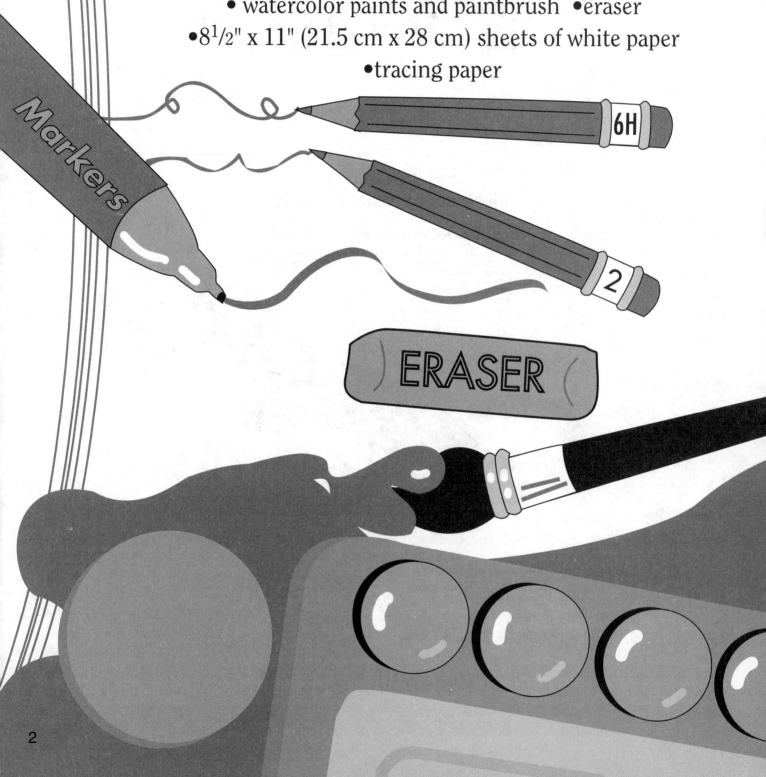

Most of the drawings in this book start with simple shapes: triangles, squares, and ovals. Begin by drawing the first steps lightly in pencil, or use the tracing paper to trace the basic shapes in the first steps. Connect the shapes, then add details, such as a nose, eyes, ears, etc. Smooth out the lines, then go over all the lines you want to keep with the black marker. Highlight fur, feathers, or other areas, then erase all the leftover pencil lines. Color your drawings with crayons or watercolor paints, or leave them in pencil.

Horse

Horses were once the main way people traveled. Today, farmers and herders use horses for work, but many people like to keep horses as pets and ride them just for fun. Horses eat all kinds of grains, grasses, and hay, but they do not eat meat.

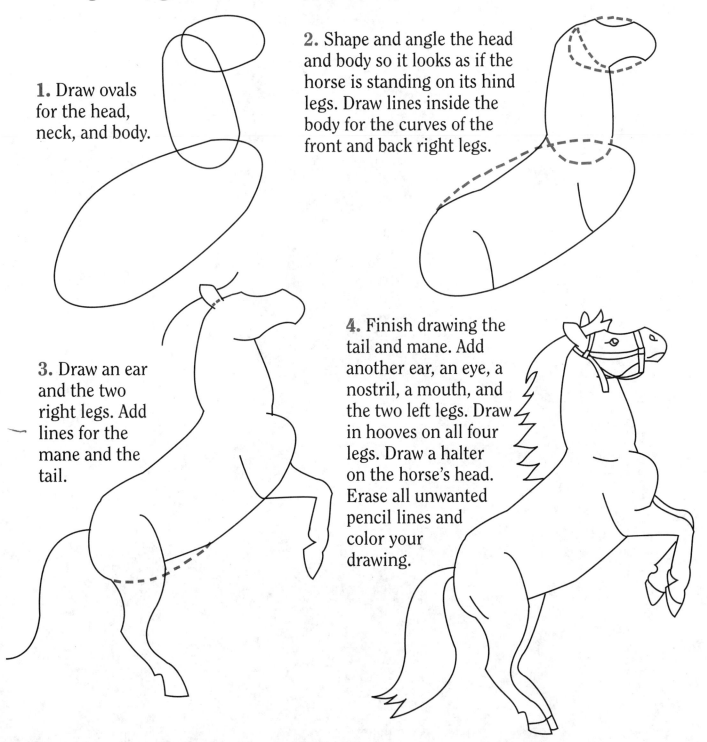

1. Draw ovals for the head, neck, and body.

2. Shape and angle the head and body so it looks as if the horse is standing on its hind legs. Draw lines inside the body for the curves of the front and back right legs.

3. Draw an ear and the two right legs. Add lines for the mane and the tail.

4. Finish drawing the tail and mane. Add another ear, an eye, a nostril, a mouth, and the two left legs. Draw in hooves on all four legs. Draw a halter on the horse's head. Erase all unwanted pencil lines and color your drawing.

Dog

Dogs are great companions—some people call them their "best friend." Dogs are color-blind, and can only see shades of gray. Their sense of smell is very developed, so dogs recognize objects by their odors instead of by shapes or colors.

1. Draw ovals for the head, ear, and body.

2. Add another ear and a front leg. Draw a curved line at the back of the body to show that the dog is sitting down. Add lines for the neck.

3. Draw back paws and a tail. Add the other front leg. Shape the face.

4. Draw the eye, nose, mouth, and tongue. Add detail to the dog's ears and paws. Draw grass and a ball for the dog to play with. Erase all unwanted pencil lines and color your drawing.

Cats and Kittens

Cats and kittens are lovable, playful pets. They "talk" to humans by using body language and making sounds. If your cat or kitten rubs against you and purrs, it is happy. If its fur stands up and it is growling, watch out!

1. Draw a large oval for the body and a small oval for the head.

2. Add legs, a tail, and an ear.

3. Add detail to the paws. Draw another ear inside the head and add details. Draw the eyes and nose.

4. Draw whiskers. Add detail to the eyes. Erase all unwanted pencil lines and color your drawing.

Parakeets

These small birds make great pets because they are friendly and lovable. Parakeets are also very colorful—their feathers can be green, red, blue, orange, yellow, or purple! Adult male parakeets have a bluish patch above their beaks, and females have a brownish patch.

1. Draw an oval for the wing area. Draw a half-oval with a curve for the head and body. Draw a rounded rectangle for the tail.

2. Draw a beak and an eye. Start defining the feathers.

3. Add details to the beak and feathers. Draw feet. Draw a branch for the parakeet to perch on. Erase all unwanted pencil lines and color your drawing.

Canary

Canaries are popular pets because they sing lovely songs and are good companions. Most pet canaries have yellow feathers, but if you feed them red peppers their feathers could turn orange!

1. Draw a small oval for the head and a long oval for the body. Draw two lines for the legs.

2. Draw eyes, the wing outline, and the feet. Shape the head.

3. Draw a beak and the tail.

4. Add feathers to the wing and tail. Add detail to the head. Erase all unwanted pencil lines and color your drawing.

Rabbits

A rabbit's eyes are on the sides of its head. This helps the rabbit to better see behind and to the sides. A rabbit's teeth are always growing. Put a piece of wood in your rabbit's cage. The rabbit will gnaw on it and wear down its teeth.

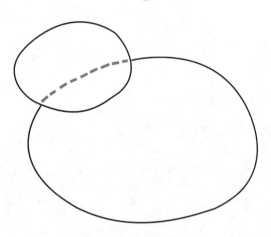

1. Draw a large oval for the body and a small oval for the head.

2. Shape the head by smoothing out the lines. Draw the ears and the back leg line.

3. Draw an eye and the front and back paws. Draw the mouth and nose. Add detail to the ears.

4. Add details to the face, including whiskers. Draw grass for the rabbit to sit in. Erase all unwanted pencil lines and color your drawing.

Goldfish

Goldfish have no eyelids. If you keep them as pets, be sure the tank is in a shady spot. As some kinds of goldfish grow, they can develop many different colors.

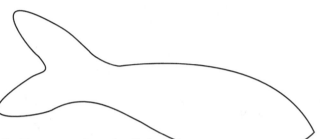

1. Draw a simple fish shape with a tail.

1. Draw a simple fish shape with a curved tail.

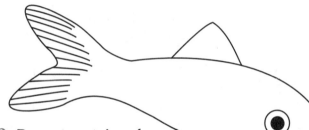

2. Draw two triangles for the fins. Draw an eye. Add detail to the tail.

2. Draw two triangles for the fins. Draw an eye and a gill line. Add detail lines to the tail.

3. Add detail to the fins and the body. Draw some air bubbles around the goldfish. Erase all unwanted pencil lines and color your drawing.

3. Add detail to the fins and body. Draw some air bubbles around the goldfish. Erase all unwanted pencil lines and color your drawing.

Tropical Fish

Most tropical fish are a little smaller than goldfish. The most common tropical fish is the guppy. Male guppies have beautiful colors, but female guppies are usually gray.

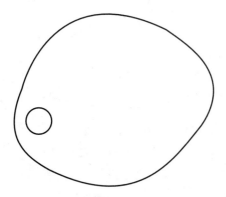

1. Draw a fat oval. Add a circle for the eye.

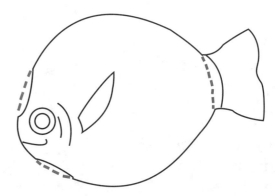

2. Shape the front of the fish. Add detail to the body. Draw the tail.

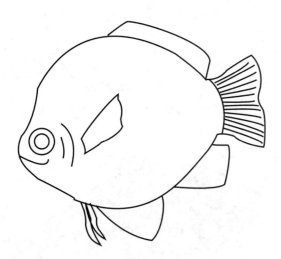

3. Draw the fins. Add detail to the tail.

4. Add more detail to the body. Draw some air bubbles around the fish. Erase all unwanted pencil lines and color your drawing.

Spotted Salamanders

The spotted salamander lives in the woods and eats mainly worms and insects. It has dark skin with yellow spots. This makes it hard for other animals to see the spotted salamander.

1. Draw a large oval for the body and a small oval for the head.

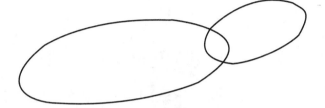

2. Draw the eyes, tail, and legs.

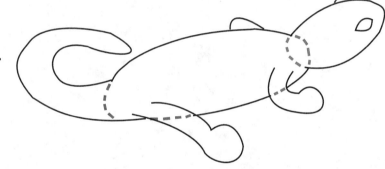

3. Add toes to the front and back feet. Add detail to one eye.

4. Draw spots all over the salamander. Erase all unwanted pencil lines and color your drawing.

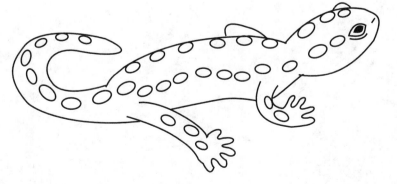

Frog

Most frogs have long back legs that help them jump far. When a frog is hungry, it uses its sticky tongue to catch insects. Frogs spend part of their lives living in water.

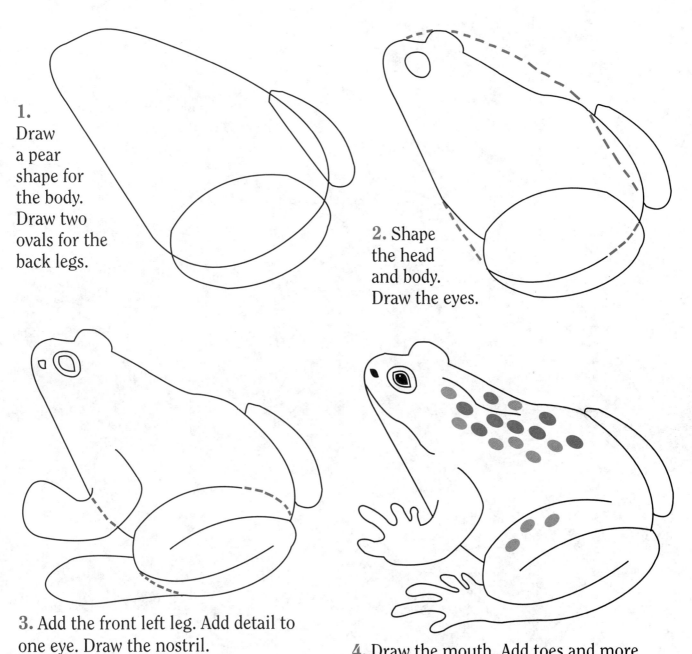

1. Draw a pear shape for the body. Draw two ovals for the back legs.

2. Shape the head and body. Draw the eyes.

3. Add the front left leg. Add detail to one eye. Draw the nostril.

4. Draw the mouth. Add toes and more detail to the eye. Add detail to the body. Erase all unwanted pencil lines and color your drawing.

Turtle

Turtles are the only reptiles that have shells. If a turtle feels it is in danger, it will pull its head and legs into its shell. Most turtles eat both plants and animals.

1. Draw a large oval for the body and a small oval for the head. Draw a rounded triangle for the tail.

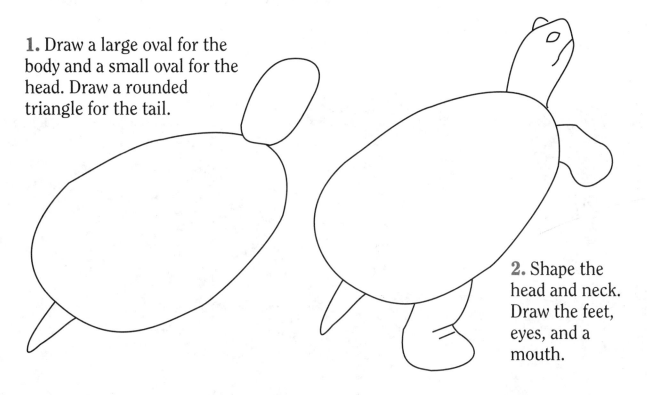

2. Shape the head and neck. Draw the feet, eyes, and a mouth.

3. Draw detail on the shell. Add detail to one eye. Draw claws on the feet. Erase all unwanted pencil lines and color your drawing.

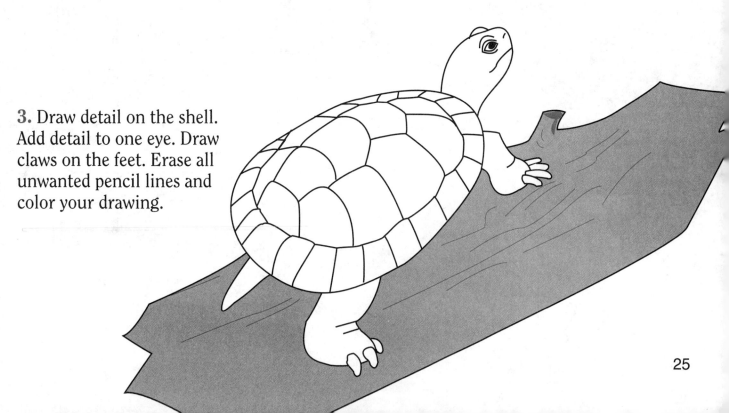

Ducks

Baby ducks are called ducklings. Most ducklings can swim when they are born. They cannot fly until a few weeks later. Male ducks are called drakes, and female ducks are called ducks. All ducks have webbed feet and waterproof feathers.

Adult duck

1. Draw a large oval for the body and a small oval for the head. Draw two lines under the body for the legs.

2. Shape the front of the head into the bill. Draw an eye. Add a wing. Begin drawing the feet.

3. Draw the feathers. Add more detail to the bill, body, and feet. Erase all unwanted pencil lines and color your drawing.

Duckling

1. Draw a small oval for the body and a smaller oval for the head. Draw two lines under the body for the legs.

2. Soften the edges of the ovals. Draw a wing on the body. Draw an eye and a small bill. Draw the feet. Erase all unwanted pencil lines and color your drawing.

Hamsters

Hamsters eat many kinds of food. They like fruit, raw vegetables, some meat, oats, and small grains. Hamsters like to play at night.

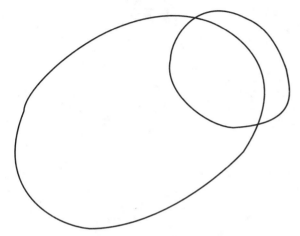

1. Draw a large oval for the body and a small oval for the head.

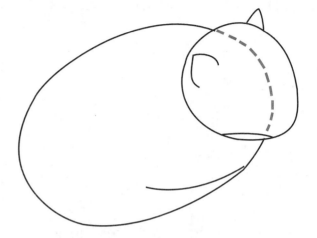

2. Shape the head and draw ears. Draw a line on the body for the front right leg.

3. Add detail to the ears. Draw an eye. Draw toes on the front leg and the back legs.

4. Smooth out the body lines so they look furry. Add detail to the eye. Draw another front paw. Draw food for the hamster to eat. Draw hay under the hamster. Erase all unwanted pencil lines and color your drawing.

Ant Farm

Ants are called social insects because they live in groups. Ants are hard workers and very strong. They can lift objects that are ten times their own weight.

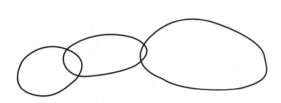

1. Draw three small ovals for the body and head.

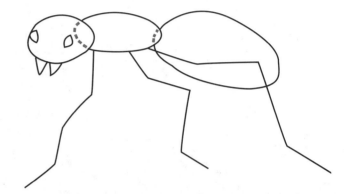

2. Draw the eyes and mandibles. Draw three legs.

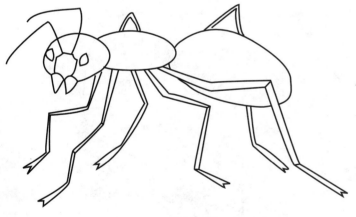

3. Add detail to the legs. Draw the last three legs. Draw the antennae on the ant's head.

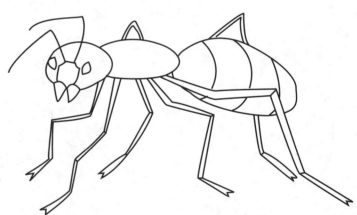

4. Add detail to the body. Erase all unwanted pencil lines and color your drawing.

Iguana

Most iguanas live in deserts or dry places. A few kinds of iguanas live in tropical rain forests. Green iguanas have a large flap of skin under their throats called a dewlap.

1. Draw a large oval for the body and a small oval for the head. Draw an eye.

2. Add detail to the eye. Draw the mouth and some scales on the back of the iguana's head. Draw the legs.

3. Draw the feet and toes. Draw the tail. Draw claws on the ends of the toes. Draw the dewlap under the iguana's throat. Draw scales on the iguana's back. Erase all unwanted pencil lines and color your drawing.

$1.95 U.S.
$2.75 CAN.

Drawing your favorite pet is easy and fun! The step-by-step directions in this book will show you how to draw dogs, cats, and other special pets.

Look for all the How to Draw books:

Baby Animals
Birds
Boats, Trains, and Planes
Cars and Trucks
Cartoon Characters
Cats
The Circus
Clowns
Dinosaurs
Dogs
Fairy Tale Characters
Farm Animals

Flowers
Forest Animals
Funny Animals
Funny People
Ghosts, Goblins, and Witches
Horses
Indian Arts and Crafts
Monsters, Weirdoes & Aliens
Prehistoric Animals
Sea Creatures
Wild Animals
Zoo Animals

ISBN 0-8167-2743-0

50195

9 780816 727438

Watermill Press